Foreign Forays

Poems of Travel in Europe and the Med

Antony Johae

Foreign Forays
published in the United Kingdom in 2025
by Mica Press & Campanula Books

c/o Leslie Bell
47 Belle Vue Road, Wivenhoe, Colchester, Essex CO7 9LD
micapress.uk | contact@micapress.uk

ISBN 978-1-869848-39-2
Copyright © Antony Johae 2025

The right of Antony Johae to be identified as the author of this work has been asserted by him in accordance with the Copyright, Designs and Patents Act of 1988.

All rights reserved.

For my brother, Tim, who loved to travel.

Acknowledgements

My thanks to the editors of the following publications in which versions of some of these poems have appeared: *Essex Belongs to Us: Writing about the real Essex* (Amazon, 2017), *The Frogmore Papers*, *George Crabbe Poetry Competition Anthology* (Suffolk Poetry Society, 2018), *The High Window*, *The Journal*, *London Grip New Poetry*, *Orbis*, *Poetry Plus*, *Poetry Salzburg Review*, *The Recusant*, *Stone's Throw: art from poetry / poetry from art* (Mosaic Stanza, 2016), *Temenos Academy Review*, *Towards the Light: poems of reconciliation* (Kapaju Books, 2018), *The Transnational*, and *Twelve Rivers Magazine* (Suffolk Poetry Society),

'My Acupuncturist's Last Words' appeared as 'Dr Hu's Last Words' in Antony Johae's *Poems of the East* (Gipping Press, 2015). 'Arrival at Rafik Hariri International Airport, Beirut' appeared in the same collection.

Thanks also to members of the *Mosaic* Stanza of the Poetry Society for critiquing some of the poems; to Marie-Luise Schnackenburg for the German translation of 'At the Museum of the History of Polish Jews'; to Sally Festing for editing 'Refugee at Calais' and to Brenda Jones for providing her painting, 'Sorrento', for the front cover.

Finally, my thanks to Leslie Bell at Mica Press for his editorial advice on the journey to publication.

Introduction

In 1940, when I was nearly three years old, my parents, together with my grandparents and my baby brother, moved from London to get away from the German bombing of the capital. The remainder of the war years were spent in the peaceful atmosphere of Henley-on-Thames. But from an early age, London drew me, as though I were destined to travel once I had grown up. The first poem, "My First Bike", reflects this incipient *Wanderlust*.

In September 1945, four months after the war had ended, I was packed off to a boarding school and spent the next ten years travelling intermittently between home and school. Travel of this kind felt penal and inspired no poetry.

It was not until I left college, and when Colchester, in north east Essex, became my home town, that I was able to pack my bag and launch out on inspired travel to Europe and beyond. This is reflected in the second poem, "Staring through My Window in Winter".

Some of the "journeys" are imaginary. The poem, "Burnt Sorrento", is an ekphrastic response to a painting by Brenda Jones which appears on the front cover of this book, while "French Toast" ironically pays tribute to the EU workings of Brussels and Strasbourg. The majority of the poems, however, are based on the experience of actual travel; these generally tell a story and are written in narrative mode.

Whether actual or imagined, *Foreign Forays* takes the reader on a diverse excursion to places as far apart as Bruges and Beirut and as near as Prague and Warsaw.

Bon voyage!

My First Bike

Down Deanfield Avenue I ride over a stony way
– corrugated iron fence to the left, orchard to the right –
on the unmade road.

Big boys, jeering, hold me up and grab my cap.
They knock me off; I cry over my scratched bike.
The boys banter and amble up the Avenue
leaving me with a stinging knee and a dirty cap.

I won't go home to seek solace from my mother
nor ointment for the graze.
I'll ride on to town – past school and gasworks –
making for the station and a ticket to the junction.
Then, from the platform, I'll see the London trains roar by.

Staring through My Window in Winter

There's a tree with ivy coiling up;
from my sick-bed it seems like a slow strangulation;
there's another topped by a crow's nest, empty now the season's out.
Greyfriars, where my mother went to school, is boarded up
its walled garden consigned to cars and traders' vans.
A low sun unfreezes the frost where the tarmac is touched by it,
but under the wall's long shadow the white will last through to the night.
Beyond I see coloured tops of buses crawling up to town
or plunging down to Eastgates and the weedy waters of the Colne.

Through the top pane the sky is plain blue,
an emptiness – until a white trail traces a way across it
– and another and another – through the afternoon.
I think of home passages looking down at the Blackwater,
the sight of the islands – Mersea, Osea, and Ray –
estuary and withied creeks, sanctuaries and purple saltings,
and – losing height – strips of rich soil plotted and pieced
before the mass of London's grey conurbations
– all seen from a window seat.

Here in the deep-blue-dusk
my mind's full of flights – those taken to far places,
on assignation, new-found family, contract or recreation.
Outside the trees are turning silhouette,
a last blackbird twitters home,
the old school, bereft of pupils, is still,
a cold driver tries to start his car.
I get up to draw the warm curtains,
see my case, lid open, beckoning me to pack.

From Bruges to Brubeck

It was grey autumn on Flanders' flats;
colours did not stand out, nor sharp city lines
give shape to what Van Eyce had seen.
No shadows led early walkers west
nor followed in the slow evening
– and when Belfort bells rang out, I thought I heard
a kind of *Liebestod*,[1] prelude to the hour.

I wandered lonely in a drizzle with the crowd,
past *Sint Gilliskerk*, on up to old *St. Jacques*
and at *Sint Anna* saw racked Jesus peeling in a niche
yellow notices pinned dog-eared to a board
soggy moss lining the pile's footings
the church a mass of bricks ready for cement
with the West Door shut.

I took shelter from the rain in a gallery,
viewed Monique de Rae's "Blue-Eyed Lady"
but saw only a dog centred in every picture
signifying such a life, I thought;
then passed from museum to museum:
Groeninge, *Gruuthuse*, *Volkskunde*, and *Lace*,
but felt no beating heart.

The rain easing, I saw them as I turned a canal corner,
four musicians on a platform ready to play –
and when they started, the clouds seemed to separate
to the rhythm of their raggy waltz
the light giving rhyme to their riffs
to the piano's counterpoint
to the sax's syncopations
the bass man's fingered time
the swish-swish of percussion brushes
– and with it, the city took on
its lost colour, staggering line,
and I could see through Van Eyce's eyes again.

[1] German – 'love-death'

Bruges Interlude

Stopping for a beer at a hostel in Bruges I met them:
three African men, the oldest, once from Congo, sacristan at St. Anna's,
so long there that as he gave his charity speech to the small gathering
I thought I heard an unblemished Flemish;
a young Ugandan on the run from his government, penniless,
mired in bureaucratic slough waiting for a permit to work
who bent towards me for commiseration in the happy room;
the third, lambasting Africa's mess, had boated from Cameroonian coast
and now with his papers straight and settled into a safe state,
welded on a building site for a Euro-handsome wage.
I think of Ghana – my full years there, teacher of British classics
– Smollett, Swift, Richardson and Sterne – with shop shelves empty,
four gallons a week, discontent and a coup d'état.
When the dancers came in – local girls of fair flesh in slinky black
with partners who knew what they were talking about –
our heads were turned. The music cutting into our conversation
I drained my glass, slipped out into the cool air
and left them gyrating to salsa.
At Legon[1] campus gates. Pass through hands held, my wife, daughters,
to palmed avenue, pantile roofs – such an ecstasy – home, home,
a hill up to bougainvillea, chancellor's house, view to Achimota, sink into a happiness . . .
but suddenly I sense their indifference – and wake up.

---

[1] University of Ghana, Accra.

From a Train Window

Yellow-blue circus
tent, striped, motley crowd outside,
set in Flanders field.

A Day in Leuven

The sun dazzled down on pastoral flats
one leisurely Saturday on a Belgian train
skimming past poplar rows, low-slung farm houses,
ogee-curved roof-tiles a startling-red in the mead,
and through the glass in an instant
I saw a tent striped in circus yellow and blue
with a motley wedding crowd outside,
surely a picture to be painted
or turned into seventeen tight syllables.

In Astrid Park I saw them,
a child pushed by his tired mother,
like Sterne's starling, wanting to get out;
couples enamoured by the day
locked in talk or eager arms;
a gorgeous girl hobbling on high heels
along the cobbled park path;
a bright ball bounced past my bench
I, like a manager, as the players pursued;
a bent pensioner fed pigeons,
they grabbed at the crumbs of this work-worn man
I tucking into my scrumptious buns
bought in the morning from a bakery in Bruges.

There's an ample square where students lounge in cafés
talking loudly in the evening;
you can smell the smoke of their cigarettes and the tang of strong coffee.
Here, in a corner, I sit writing my country haiku, revising my clouded elegy.
I have seen the slanted sun lose itself behind a stepped gable,
the square descend into shadow, café lights coming on discretely;
heard the great clock strike another hour, the church clang out its call to service,
a riot of young voices rising into the night. I have finished writing,
drink the last of my spun-out tea, beckon the waiter to pay, tip as befits him,
and leaving the teeming square, make for the station.

The way was late-calm, shops shut up,
only the thump-thump of a late music boutique
or car purring close past me
broke into the tiredness of my mind,
until at the station square
the four-four time of a tango stopped me
staccato-wise in the street.
I saw the dancers in dark dress glide past
with café people looking on in fascination,
long measured steps seeming like giant strides
punctuated by late pauses, legs stretched,
heads held in near embrace –
then pivots into fresh directions across the paving floor.

On the train I see myself in the glass
get up from my second-class seat
brush aside my finished glass
draw up to her, dark-haired Argentinian,
hold her hard around the waist
and to plucked notes and piano chords
accordion blasts and sweeping strings
set off in supple dance.

My Acupuncturist's Last Words

You said not to hate winter –
to put up with shivering showers,
to relish churlish winds,
stand up to influenza's grip,
feel free in trussed up clothes
– you said not to hate a thing.

This mid-summer, camping in Calais –
rain rattling on the van roof,
west wind funneling furiously
down the Channel, I leaning into it
as I went to get fresh bread for breakfast;
and on Flanders roads, the sight of my umbrella
soaked on the van's rusty floor,
the sound of wipers wearing down,
and through the glass the constant grey of flat sky
– how I loved everything!

Refugee at Calais

He was at the basin when I entered,
stopped shaving, made way apologetically,
mumbled a word in English, then in French
while I washed my hands before breakfast
at the quayside *boulangerie*.[1]

Confiture[2] had made my hands sticky, butter and croissant greasy.

He was still at the basin when I went back.
"*Encore ici!*"[3] I said in surprise – he seemed to take fright,
packed up his shaving things –
"It is not sharp," he said, makeshift razor in hand.
I would have gifted him a fresh blade, but had shaved electric on 240 volts
at the municipal camp site where my wife and daughter slept.

As I went back to the comfort of my bunk
I thought of him returning to the camp they called *La Jungle*
– to a half-shelter of plastic, pumped water, squalid washing and despair –
razed by the town *gendarmerie*[4] days after we took the easy ferry to Dover,
an erasure which, like the man's face, would not stay long smooth.

---

[1] French – bakery
[2] French - jam
[3] French – "Still here!"
[4] French – police

Wandering, Wondering

I wandered lonely as a tourist
in a crowded seaside village.
It was Sunday in high August
with church bells ringing
when all at once I saw a cloud,
like a ghost or apparition, threatening
outburst. It lay across the bay
hanging heavily on the water
tossing it in a sort of dance.
I gazed: a poet could not but wonder
as when one sees first flowers show.
It dripped; awnings of gift shops flapped
gust driven; drops touched the tarmac
glistening it; tourist folk filled cafés
while bells rang out another refuge.

Inside was dark like Kafka's cathedral,
sounds solemn, the congregation old.
Candles flickered about to be snuffed out,
incense rose and hung with figures in the vault.
Was für eine Stille herrschte jetzt im Dom! [1]
It was unkind and cold.
I followed the stations wondering
at the broken corpse unnailed, the woman
holding it. She fell on my shoulder
(I on the stone) moaning white-faced and wet.
I (on unprayerful knees) reached out
to forestall her fall, grasped her coarse dress
to take the toppling weight
– and pewed her.

I was now the woman's pillow leant on by provision
a prop, a stay, a strut, upholder even
though her breath still rattled, staving off
Death. "*Quelle chaleur!*"[2]

The floor was fridge-cold.
I felt shivers in the draught
pictured rigor mortis.
To feel the heat in this uncanny tomb!
She loosened the scarf around her neck,
touched my hand: there was heat in it!
I wondered at such warmth so close to expiring.
It was as kisses bring back breath from the threshold.
What had not changed was the floor set in stone
but there'd been a sublimation: I did not feel alone.

Cancale, Britanny

---

[1] German – Quoted from Franz Kafka's novel, *Der Prozess* (*The Trial*): What stillness there was now in the Cathedral!
[2] French – It's so hot!

French Toast

It was to be a breakfast meeting of the ministers:

On the table – *Brötchen,*[1] *Wurst,*[2] and cheese; smoked red herring; *croissant* and *confiture;*[3] Danish pastries and French toast; *latte, café crème,*[4] tea, and organic juices.

Also on the table – a proposal on agricultural policy to be agreed by the parties; but the French had found fault with it and threatened veto.

The charming Italian minister, who was now yawning, had been busy during the night working on the chief French negotiator; a slight amendment had been announced and agreement achieved.

When the breakfast had been consumed and the papers were brought in to be signed, elegant glasses were placed on the tables and bottles of Champagne wheeled in on a silver trolley.

Uncorked, the Commissioner delivered a congratulatory speech, during which time the waiters poured out the Champagne.

"Finally," he concluded, "I would like to make special mention of the Minister from France who, after some misgivings, has seen his way to approving the accord. To him I would like to propose a toast. A toast to the French!" he said raising his glass.

"To the French!"

---

[1] German – bread roll
[2] German – sausage
[3] French – jam
[4] French – coffee with cream

Elements

Notre Dame on fire
consumed before Easter
volcano of heat.
Firemen hose it
to put it out.
Will the Cathedral fall to earth
or be raised again into the air?

From Above

It was once an arsenal
then under the hand of royal engineers
a tower rose from the roof,
Chausey granite housing heavy bells.
Through the Great Porch, the Great Organ
rests on monolithic pillars
weighty as those the ancient judge dislodged.
Four prophets hand out warnings at the pulpit,
four Evangelists point to "the Devil crushed."

The Introit bids us take the hand of God:
Voici le temps, le temps
où Dieu fait grace à notre terre.[1]
But then Wisdom is read :
Nous avons peine à nous représenter ce qui est sur terre,
et nous trouvons avec effort ce qui est à portée de la main;
qui donc a découvert ce qui est dans les cieux?[2]
God's grandeur is the psalmist's song:
Tu fait retourner l'homme à la poussière . . .
Tu les as balayés.[3]

With such words am I swept along
like a swirling leaf in a swollen stream
where no grace is
nor any kind hand to cup me.
Of such weight is the ministry
I am pulled down.
This ancient pile totters
or why the scaffold where weekday workmen
do a mason's job on powerless pillars
in vain restoration?

Did the Pantheon last, or Pilate's palace?
They are just swept up dust.
Now I feel it falling but for the scaffold's embrace.
My skull aches with the weight.
Then high on a platform I see something that secures me:
a hard hat.

L'église Sainte-Croix de Saint-Servan, Brittany

[1] Now is the time, the time
when God gives grace to our earth.

[2] We have difficulty in figuring out what goes on on earth,
and of grasping what is to hand;
who then is able to comprehend what is in the heavens?

[3] You will return man to dust . . .
He will be swept up.

Prague Swing

        At the Teatro Musicale in the Municipal House, Prague
        there's a concert for four saxes
                Jazz on a summer's night.
                      Bohemian players bend to sinuous instruments:
              Pavel puffs windingly on soprano and tenor
    little Roman coils notes on light alto, and lithe
    Katerina leans bearing fat baritone.
                They're ranged on stage to begin Bozza's *Andante* and *Scherzo*
    Bernstein's swaying suite from the West Side, and
Drevikovsky's *Funny Tones for Saxophones*:
Ein Wiener Tanz, Blues Pastorale, Mazurka, Intermezzo, and Cake-Walk Dance.

                      After Entr'acte – Iturralde, Piazzolla and Gershwin:
              Suite Helenica: Kalamatianos, Funky, Vals, Kritis;
    Night Club 1960 from *Histoire du Tango*, and eliding whine of
Rhapsody in Blue to wrap the music up
        – all this to curvaceous *Obecni Dum - Vinarna*
            in swindling July.

Lebanese Lapse

I am in a northern European cathedral town
one wet summer, on the road to a lost love.

The streets are clotted with cars. Parking's prohibitive
and I'm circling for luck in my old VW van.

Finding it out, I take recourse to the multi-storey,
descend to dungeon dark, but spot no space in this chancy lot.

I keep turning, turning on a downward gyre,
take tight bends, sweating sans power steering,

returning again and again to replica levels.
Panic at sudden *Ausgang*,[1]

take a turn against the oil-smeared arrow,
find I'm up against cars with affronted drivers.

I realize my Lebanese lapse and rue it,
caught, it seems, in a Dantesque trap.

In a slow revolution, steering's lugged
left and right and left . . . old arms ache.

Now I'm wheeling again past taken spaces.
Fall into a funnel, destined for infernal circles.

Münster, Germany

[1] German – Exit

At the Museum of the History of Polish Jews

It lies in Zamenhota Street in Warsaw restored,
stained city of brick-walled ghetto
where those of Abraham's progeny found themselves locked in,
ignorant of onward transit to camps and chambers.
I follow their story after Jerusalem's fall to Roman ruination,
their wanderings west, their finding rest on *Polin*'s[1] prosperous plain.
Here they waxed tolerably well in *Paradisus Iudaecorum*[2]
until hellish pogroms saw them chased and chastised,
their gentle gardens routed, race despised.
Not long, and Poland, too, was parted
by triple-powered Russia, Austria, and Prussia.
Came the Great War, and the peace to end all peace,
Polish nation resurrected, white-and-red flag raised;
not long – lowered to Adolf's hateful Swastika,
land for *Lebensraum*[3] impressed, purge of Polish Jews renewed.
I read of their entrapment, enactment of slaughter;
see a couple clasp their daughter – a child – as the gas pours in.

In Zamenhota Street there's a monument to this sorry suffering;
ribbons and wreaths lie strewn over dark steps
– ribbons blue and white, wreaths crowned with David's star.
I hear a woman weeping, young in the dying day;
she crouches and cries while others casually pass by.
I think her lost ones could once have lived here
before a terrible train took them to Treblinka.
Now the seven-candled flame flickers and is out.
I mount the monument steps and see among the blue and white
the woman's wreath, her wretched ribbon white and red,
Polish tears for the Jewish dead.

[1] Hebrew – Poland [or] rest here
[2] Latin – Paradise of the Jews
[3] German – living space [for Germans]

Im Museum der Geschichte der polnischen Juden

Es liegt in der Zamenhota Straße im wieder aufgebauten Warschau,
befleckte Stadt des mit Ziegeln ummauerten Ghettos,
wo Abrahams Nachkommen sich eingeschlossen fanden,
nichtsahnend vom Weitertransport in die Lager und Kammern.
Ich folge ihrer Geschichte nach dem Fall Jerusalems bis zur Zerstörung Roms,
ihren Wanderungen nach Westen, bis sie Ruhe fanden auf *Polins* fruchtbaren Ebenen.
Hier im *Paradisus Iudaecorum* blühten sie leidlich auf
bis höllische Pogrome sie gejagt und gezüchtigt sahen,
ihre schönen Gärten vernichtet, ihre Rasse verachtet.
Nicht lange danach, und auch Polen wurde geteilt
von der dreifachen Macht Russland, Österreich und Preußen.
Es kam der Große Krieg, und der Friede, der allen Frieden beendigte,
die polnische Nation erhob sich wieder, die weiß-rote Flagge wurde gehisst;
nicht lange, niedergeholt vor Hitlers verhasster Swastika,
das Land beschlagnahmt für ‚Lebensraum', die Säuberung von polnischen Juden wieder aufgenommen.
Ich lese von ihrer Überlistung, der Anordnung zum Abschlachten;
sehe ein Paar ihre Tochter – ein Kind – umklammern, als das Gas einströmt.

In der Zamenhota Straße steht ein Denkmal für dieses traurige Leiden;
Bänder und Kränze liegen verstreut auf dunklen Stufen
– blaue und weiße Bänder, Kränze bekrönt vom Davidstern.
Ich höre eine Frau weinen, eine junge Frau am verlöschenden Tag;
sie kauert und weint, während andere gleichgültig vorbeigehen.
Ich stelle mir vor, dass ihre Verlorenen hier einmal gelebt haben könnten
bevor ein furchtbarer Zug sie nach Treblinka brachte.
Jetzt flackert die Flamme des siebenarmigen Leuchters und geht aus.
Ich steige die Stufen des Denkmals hoch und sehe unter dem Blau und Weiß
den Kranz der Frau, ihr armseliges weißes und rotes Band,
polnische Tränen für die jüdischen Toten.

Translated by Marie-Luise Schnackenburg

In the Men's Room at the Fryderyk Chopin Museum, Warsaw

This tap's a teaser;
it doesn't spout,
water simply won't come out.
I press hard with no result;
it feels almost like insult.
I try turning the knob from right to left
and am left bereft.
Is there a key to this stubborn faucet?
If not, I'll be driven to force it.
By "key", I don't mean C major or F minor
the kind you find on a maestro's *Steinway*
but rather a trick or flick or stamp or jerk
that would make the blinking thing work.
I think, perchance, this tap may turn it*self* on;
I put my unsoaped palms under, but water – none!
I ask a Japanese man to try
but he's as nonplussed as I.
He turns the tap and twists it
but still it perfidiously resists.
Now he's pulling the knob toward him
back and forth as though training at a gym.
Then, at a whim, hot liquid comes out in a rush
– it showers both of us.
Is the dryer working? No.
I tell the Japanese man it's time to go,
to leave this teasing tap alone.
He assents and exits wiping his soaked phone.

Building Ironies (for Pawel)

In Warsaw's Szucha Street stands a twenties structure raised for religion.
In '39, when German tanks swarmed in, the Gestapo laid hands on it.
Inside, innocents would wait on "tram" benches facing forwards.
They'd be bullied, bull-whipped, and bitten by dogs, prelude to interrogation.
Come enlightened times, this is the site of Poland's Ministry of Education.

In Ujazdowskie Street lies a princely palace where post-war Poland
saw torture augmented: Beatings with truncheon, rod, stick, and whip.
Burning of the eye with cigarette. Plucking of hair from head, chest, crotch
and scrotum. With the fall of the Wall and the end of secret service tyranny
this place now houses the Polish Justice Ministry.

In Jerozolimskie Street rises an austere edifice
once the United Workers Party headquarters.
When the one party fell, the building still stood.
Under the new dispensation, as though to compensate the regime's shortchange,
there was a conversion – into the capital's Stock Exchange.

Maqam[1] in the Park of Baths (for Faruk)

You played your nine-reed Ney
in Warsaw's Park of Baths, under September sun
before a classic pile. Had there been words
they would have been of love – beauty
glistening like the lake; parting pain, a drowning.

You played your seven-curtained Ney
at the palace on the isle, by the water's edge
with people passing. Had there been words
they would have heard of love – spotless,
soaring sunward; unrequited, dragged to earth.

You played notes of sweet semi-tone on Ney,
your listener, Antony, to Sufi ghazal[2]
before a royal residence. Had there been words
you would have sung of love – of Rumi's rapture
and Hafez sore-yearning for his bride.

---

[1] Arabic – literally, place; in Arabic music, the system of melodic modes.
[2] Arabic, Persian, Urdu - an oriental poem, or song, of love and loss written in a particular form.

Rome Poem

They say when in Rome do as the Romans
but I don't see many to ape.
It is Bangladeshi boys who herd the foreign hordes
from street to touring bus or tout made-in-China souvenirs
– pietà, opener, pendant, purse –
through the melting day, martyrs to business.
When you wander in the streets or stop at crowded fountains
Africans off leaky boats hail you with their begging bowls
and bring to mind, in this excess, survival in far places.

Sitting in a roadside restaurant we hear an ill-clad man
on well-worn accordion play a joyful jazz;
his fingers race crazily, our feet beat lazily.
A black car draws up and a heavy man gets out;
he's here to check the player's papers – to move him on.
My daughter asks the waiter why?
"Romany," he says, "thieves!" and puts down full portions.
Accordion shoulder-slung, we see him pass along the street.
Without accompaniment we eat half-cooked pasta in tomato paste,
at eleven Euros a go – a waste
and wonder at such home-grown theft.
We'll dance with the Romany
but we'll not do as the Romans.

Burnt Sorrento[1]

. . . rust drips into purple
                 to blue – insurgent
as sea, cerulean . . .

      stretched-strokes green, wheat-yellow
                                  shot ochre –

bronze to olive, patch of purple
                 chalk-pink on hot-rock orange
                             splashed in high white heat . . .

gouache streaked – celeste   sienna
                  sage
                           amber
    almond

      . . . mauve-marked   brick-red-brushed   terracotta-tiled

torrid – scorched – sirocco-swept –

                 baked in burnt Sorrento.

---

[1] An ekphrasis poem: a description of a visual work of art. See the painting by Brenda Jones on the cover page. "Burnt Sorrento" originally appeared in *Stone's Throw: art from poetry / poetry from art* (Mosaic Stanza, 2016) entitled, "Colour Ensemble", together with Brenda's painting.

Post-Modern Love (after George Meredith)

With PC between them he watched France lose on *Rai Uno*
while she, eyes steadfast on Windows Live Messaging,
clicked with hand's light quiver by his head
dreadfully venomous to him, he stone-still
far from sleep's heavy measure, looking for
Love's alchemy after the slow wine
they'd shared before retiring to *Davinci's b&b*
and their flight in the morning from Fiumicino.
In the pale drug of silence, regret
scrawled itself over the room's blank wall,
he slipping into sleep while she tapped out still more messages.
At take-off he took her hand in his; but once in flight
she put on earphones plugged into the screen that severs all.

Reception

The groom with his bride enters to ululations uttered shrilly by their guests.
Women in white, pink, blue, green, purple *hijab*[1] direct them to a white throne,
she tiara-crowned, he bow-tied in black.

In the glitter of sequins the band, named *Pearl*, strikes up a strident pulse;
little girls in pretty white, others nubile, short-skirted, and dames cloth-covered
inhabit the floor. The men, at first, observe them in motion.

Accordion, violin, flute, zither, and *oud* issue from a plugged in piano,
rollicking rhythms drummed from duff and tabla
and daff's moon-shaped jingles.[2]

The couple join in, he with marital abandon, bow tie discarded, she in long train
gently. Singer with microphone circulates and serenades them,
hands of men and women clasp in a circle of dance.

From the floor's edge, mobiles mimic movement and music;
little boys – suited – pass between them in attitudes of anarchy,
leaving sedentary old to imbibe fresh juice at their tables.

Man, with hand-held camera twists, leans, crouches,
takes shots of dancers and nuptial pair
for instant transmission to screens on wide walls.
When the music stops the picture's lost – *Link failed*

Sfax, Tunisia

---

[1] Arabic –Muslim woman's head scarf
[2] *Oud* – lute; *duff* – a percussion instrument; *tabla* – two-drum percussion; *daff* – tambourine

Spinning a Tale

Passing through west Essex villages, I'm on a bus to the airport for a flight to Lebanon via Istanbul. There's a money spider on my cap. It's dangling from the peak in front of my eyes.

As I check in, it seems he's chosen to fly with me. Does it mean he'll bring me luck?

After Passport Control, we are stopped. A big black dog sniffs my bag. He's not onto my spider's money. We are let through to the Gate.

Now we're aboard and my money spider's dangling again. If he's bound for Beirut, I wonder where he'll be staying. At five-star *Phoenicia*?

El Baba's Ride[1]

He sits in a glass cube
proof against imagined assassins.
Crowds wave gay flags,
soldiers standing stern at the ready.
Tall men walk with the motor cage,
black suits, slim ties, glasses shaded.
They look left and right, front and behind
with suspicion, as though someone might pounce out
and pour lead into their visitor.

He sits, white-robed, in mid-September heat
on his way to meet Lebanon's dubious dignitaries,
church and mosque men, some to kiss his kind hands,
Catholic, Maronite, Armenian, Orthodox, Syrian,
Sunni, Shi'a, Druze assembled, but for a brief encounter.
With a million mobiles clicking
the old man waves faintly from his cube
his shoulders stooped in modern martyrdom.

My mind reaches back to a man on an ass
making his way to Jerusalem.

    Beirut

---

[1] In September 2012, Pope Benedict XVI made a three-day visit to Lebanon.

Arrival at Rafik Hariri International Airport, Beirut

The queue wasn't long for foreigners;
the other for Lebanese, guest workers
home for a few days from the Gulf,
stretched back a bit. I stood on the yellow line.

He stamped the man before me
and beckoned. "Bonjour," I said and he smiled.
I handed him my passport, he flipped through the pages.
"You are coming from Kuwait?" and I nodded.

"What is your occupation?" "I teach at the University –
English . . . English Literature."
He looked at me and then at my picture,
again at me and said:
"Shall I compare thee to a summer's day?"

Biographical Note:

Antony Johae (b.1937, Chiswick) Ph.D. (thesis: a comparative study of Dostoevsky and Kafka) has taught literature at the University of Essex and in Ghana, Tunisia and Kuwait. In 2009, he retired to Lebanon (his wife's country of origin) and has since published four collections: *Poems of the East* (Gipping Press, 2015), *After-Images: Homage to Éric Rohmer* (Poetry Salzburg, 2019), *Ex-Changes* (The High Window, 2020) and *Home Poems* (Orphean Press, 2022). Antony is an active member of the Suffolk Poetry Society and of Mosaic, the Colchester stanza of the Poetry Society. He has read at the Suffolk Poetry Festival and at Poetry in Aldeburgh. He currently divides his time between Colchester and Lebanon.

www.ingramcontent.com/pod-product-compliance
Ingram Content Group UK Ltd.
Pitfield, Milton Keynes, MK11 3LW, UK
UKHW050913040225
454604UK00010BA/106